Looking at . . .
Mussaurus

A Dinosaur from the TRIASSIC Period

THE NEW
DINOSAUR
COLLECTION

For a free color catalog describing Gareth Stevens' list of high-quality books and
multimedia programs, call 1-800-542-2595 (USA) or 1-800-461-9120 (Canada).
Gareth Stevens Publishing's Fax: (414) 225-0377.
See our catalog, too, on the World Wide Web: http://gsinc.com

Library of Congress Cataloging-in-Publication Data

Green, Tamara, 1945-
    Looking at-- Mussaurus/by Tamara Green; illustrated by
Tony Gibbons. -- North American ed.
      p. cm. -- (The new dinosaur collection)
    Includes index.
    Summary: Provides information about how the Mussaurus,
a chunky herbivore living in South America during the Triassic
Period, may have looked and behaved.
    ISBN 0-8368-1789-3 (lib. bdg.)
    1. Mussaurus--Juvenile literature. [1. Mussaurus. 2. Dinosaurs.]
I. Gibbons, Tony, ill. II. Title. III. Series.
QE862.S3G754   1997
567.913--dc21   97-584

This North American edition first published in 1997 by
Gareth Stevens Publishing
1555 North RiverCenter Drive, Suite 201
Milwaukee, Wisconsin 53212 USA

This U.S. edition © 1997 by Gareth Stevens, Inc. Created with original © 1996
by Quartz Editorial Services, 112 Station Road, Edgware HA8 7AQ U.K.

Consultant: Dr. David Norman, director of the Sedgwick Museum of Geology,
University of Cambridge, England.

Additional artwork by Clare Heronneau.

Printed in the United States of America

1 2 3 4 5 6 7 8 9 01 00 99 98 97

Looking at . . .
Mussaurus
A Dinosaur from the TRIASSIC Period

by Tamara Green

Illustrated by Tony Gibbons

THE NEW
DINOSAUR
COLLECTION

Gareth Stevens Publishing
MILWAUKEE

Contents

Introducing
Mussaurus

When scientists first discovered the skeleton of a baby **Mussaurus** (MUSS-<u>SAW</u>-RUS), they were surprised to find that it was as small as a mouse. Yet by the time this dinosaur matured, it may have grown to be twenty times the size it was when newly hatched.

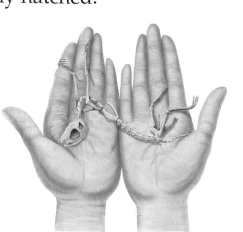

Our author and illustrator present a wealth of information about **Mussaurus** in the following pages. Have fun getting to know this recently discovered South American dinosaur, one of the rarest that paleontologists have found so far.

So what else has been discovered about this dinosaur? Where and when did **Mussaurus** live? Who named it? What was the world like way back in **Mussaurus**'s time? And, if people had existed then, would they have been frightened by this dinosaur?

Mussaurus was given its name, meaning "mouse-lizard," because the first remains discovered were mouse-like in size. But a baby **Mussaurus** would have grown to be many times larger within a few years, as you can see in this picture.

From its remains, paleontologists can tell that **Mussaurus** must have been what is known as a prosauropod. This means that it was one of the first plant-eating dinosaurs to live on Earth. This occurred in Triassic times, millions of years before the sauropods — long-necked herbivores such as **Diplodocus** (DIP-LOD-OH-KUS) — evolved.

Like all prosauropods, **Mussaurus** resembled the later sauropods in many ways, but it was smaller.

A typical prosauropod, **Mussaurus** had a small head, a long neck, a chunky body, and a long tail. Its hind limbs were thicker than the front ones, and it had five-toed feet.

lizard

Each front limb had five fingers with claws. **Mussaurus** could walk around on all fours or reach up into tall trees by standing on its sturdy back legs. If danger approached, **Mussaurus** could easily run for safety, although not very quickly. Most of the time, it just ambled along.

No one knows what color **Mussaurus** was, so the illustrator of this book has used his imagination.

Even if paleontologists do eventually find some **Mussaurus** skin, they still may not be able to tell what color it once was. But they may get an idea of how wrinkly or smooth the skin was when **Mussaurus** roamed what is now South America over 200 million years ago.

Baby

What a remarkable find it was! In the late 1970s, a group of paleontologists began digging in rocks in Patagonia, an area of southern Argentina in South America. Before long, their efforts were rewarded as they unearthed some fossilized eggs and lots of bones.

The remains were from **Mussaurus** — dinosaurs dating from Late Triassic times. This meant they were about 220 million years old.

The seven skeletons were very small — of babies, the scientists decided. In fact, they were the tiniest baby dinosaurs ever discovered. Their skulls were only 1 inch (2.5 centimeters) long, and their bodies 12 inches (30 cm) at most.

The baby dinosaurs were found huddled together in what looked like the remains of a nest. Their bones had been well preserved.

skeletons

Many people think of dinosaurs as enormous. But, of course, not all of them were huge. Some newly-hatched dinosaurs, like **Mussaurus**, were tiny.

Who would have thought that even a baby dinosaur skeleton would have been small enough to hold, millions of years later, in a human hand, as shown in the illustration on these two pages! A baby **Mussaurus** clearly had a lot of growing to do before its skeleton reached what scientists believe was probably adult size.

No one knows how or why the babies perished. Perhaps their mother died and so could not feed them; or perhaps they were too weak to survive. There may even have been more babies in the nest at first; but their miniature skeletal remains may have disintegrated with time.

9

The Late Triassic world

Earth was very different in Late Triassic times, about 220 million years ago, when dinosaurs first appeared. The world then consisted of one great ocean that scientists call Panthalassa (PAN-THAL-ASS-AH) and one huge landmass known as Pangaea (PAN-JEE-AH).

Mussaurus lived in what is now South America before this piece of land broke off from the one huge landmass. The climate was very hot then, and the landscape was dry and desertlike.

But after a rain, an oasis of seed-ferns — plants that are now extinct, just like the dinosaurs — would occasionally sprout up around pools. There were no grass or flowering plants yet. But horsetails, ginkgoes, and conifer-like trees grew in some places.

Only a few types of dinosaurs existed in Triassic times. **Mussaurus** lived peacefully most of the time alongside creatures such as salamanders, frogs, and turtles. The stillness would only be broken by the occasional roar of a carnivore as it sought its next victim or the cry of a pterosaur flying overhead.

Sometimes, too, the distant sound of an exploding volcano could be heard as it produced showers of boiling hot lava. The world was about to undergo many changes as Pangaea broke up and different continents began to form.

Mussaurus meals

Paleontologists believe that, as a typical prosauropod, **Mussaurus** would have had many small, leaf-shaped teeth lining its jaws. These teeth were ideal for biting off tough leaves and twigs. **Mussaurus** was an herbivore, so it ate only plants, not meat.

But experts think **Mussaurus**'s teeth were only used for breaking up vegetation into pieces that were small enough to be swallowed. It could not chew its food with its teeth, as you can.

How, then, did **Mussaurus** manage to grind its food and digest its meals without getting a stomachache? There is an interesting answer to that problem.

From time to time, like most prosauropods and the large sauropods that evolved millions of years later, **Mussaurus** not only ate fresh vegetation but also swallowed small stones. These would then find their way into the dinosaur's gizzard. Here, these stones, known as gastroliths, would help grind up the plant material so **Mussaurus** would not suffer from indigestion. It was an efficient way of dealing with raw plant food. Even some of today's birds and reptiles occasionally swallow stones for the same purpose.

Paleontologists have found gastroliths together with the fossilized remains of many herbivorous dinosaurs. Carnivores, however, did not need to help their digestion in this way.

Death of the hatchlings

It was the middle of a hot Triassic day, and a mother **Mussaurus** was doing her best to shelter her newly hatched babies from the scorching sun. They were tiny and had just emerged from their shells. As yet, they had small appetites, but they still needed to be fed.

Their mother would have to plod to a nearby oasis to find fresh vegetation to bring back for them. She would also be able to get a drink of water for herself.

The hatchlings were too young to run off and play yet, so the mother **Mussaurus** knew they would be safe for a while.

At the pool, she drank her fill and splashed herself with water to cool off. Feeling revived, she was about to bite off some leaves for her offsprings' lunch when the peace of the Triassic afternoon was suddenly interrupted by a loud roar.

The earliest known dinosaur, **Staurikosaurus** (STORE-EEK-OH-SAW-RUS) was a small, quick, lightly built carnivore. It was smaller than the mother **Mussaurus** but far more ferocious by nature, and it was on the lookout for lunch, too.

Taking the **Mussaurus** completely by surprise, the meat-eater sprang at her, knocking the new mother on her side. She would not survive this attack. And without her to tend and feed her hatchlings, they would not live very long, either.

Becoming a paleontologist

José F. Bonaparte, the Argentinian paleontologist who, with M. Vince, discovered **Mussaurus**, also named the dinosaurs **Carnotaurus** (CAR-NOH-TAW-RUS), **Noasaurus** (NOH-A-SAW-RUS), and **Abelisaurus** (AB-ELL-EE-SAW-RUS). These and many others were discovered in South America. Today, paleontologists are making exciting new discoveries throughout the world. They are studying and reconstructing dinosaur remains that researchers have unearthed.

What steps, then, would you need to take if you wanted to become a paleontologist? And why is studying the remains of long-extinct plants and animals considered a worthwhile job?

Most paleontologists work at natural history museums and sometimes also go on expeditions to hunt for dinosaur fossils. They begin the pursuit of their profession by studying zoology or geology at a university. But even if you do not decide to spend all your working life looking for fossils, you could still have paleontology as a hobby and go on occasional fossil-hunting trips during vacations.

Paleontologists do very interesting and important work. They help create a picture of the history of plant and animal life on Earth. Dinosaurs inhabited our world for more than 150 million years before they died out. Humans, however, have only been here for a fraction of that length of time.

Perhaps by investigating how dinosaurs lived and why they became extinct, paleontologists may also learn how to look after our planet more carefully for future generations so that *we* do not eventually become a lost species.

Dinosaur

Most dinosaur remains have vanished over millions of years, never to be seen again. They may have been eaten by scavenging creatures, become broken up in the soil, or decayed naturally. But we are lucky that some, like those *below,* have survived in the form of fossils, usually preserved in rock.

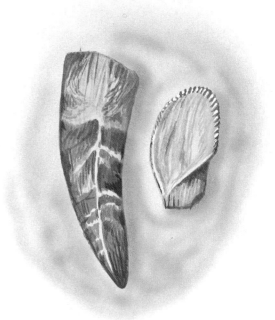

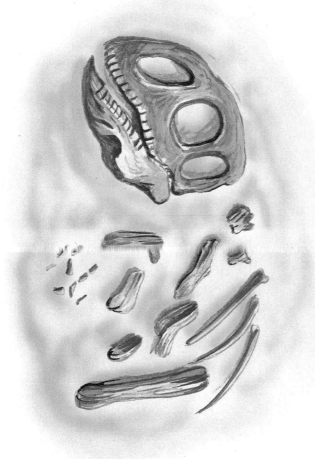

The dinosaurs' soft body parts disintegrated over time after they died. But their teeth and skeletons sometimes were protected in sand or mud, and they hardened. Minerals even turned some bones to stone; or bones themselves disappeared, leaving their shape behind as a hollow mold. Skin impressions can also be found in rock; and dinosaur teeth that have hardly changed at all — such as those *above* — have even been discovered.

fossils

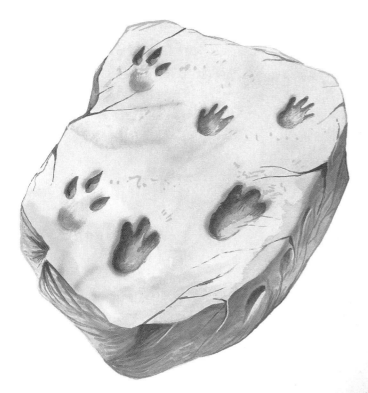

Coprolites, shown *below*, are fossilized droppings. Even though a coprolite is ancient, scientists can still tell the content of a dinosaur's diet and therefore whether it was an herbivore or carnivore. Scientists can also tell how old many fossils are by studying the layers of rock in which they have been found and by measuring the radioactivity level of the fossils.

There are other types of dinosaur fossils, too. From fossil footprints (*above*), for example, scientists can tell whether a particular dinosaur walked on two or four feet, how fast it could run, and whether it lived in herds or alone.

Meet the

Scientists have found some remarkably early dinosaur remains in South America, southern Africa, China, Tibet, North America, and Europe. Among them are a number of dinosaurs that belong to the plateosaurid (PLAT-EE-OH-SAW-RID) family — some of the very first dinosaurs to appear on our planet. They were all plant-eaters with small heads, long necks, bulky bodies, and long tails. Triassic **Mussaurus** (1) was one of these and so far has only been found in Argentina.

Triassic **Plateosaurus** (PLAT-EE-OH-SAW-RUS) (2) — reaching 26 feet (8 meters) in length and with a name meaning "flat lizard" — was discovered in western Europe.

Many skeletal remains of Triassic **Euskelosaurus** (YOU-SKEL-OH-SAW-RUS) (3), whose name means "primitive leg lizard," have been found in southern Africa.

1

2

long-necks

Fossilized bones of **Lufengosaurus** (LOO-<u>FENG</u>-OH-<u>SAW</u>-RUS) **(4)**, which was about the same height as **Euskelosaurus**, were discovered in China and Tibet. This dinosaur was a family member, but it did not evolve until a few million years later in Early Jurassic times. Like all of its plateosaurid relatives, it had teeth ideally suited to chopping up vegetation.

Then there was **Massospondylus** (<u>MASS</u>-OH-SPON-<u>DEE</u>-LOOS) **(5)**, which was a bit bigger than **Mussaurus**. It also did not appear until Early Jurassic times and roamed what is now southern Africa, as **Euskelosaurus** had done long before it. The plateosaurids were certainly a widely traveled family, and you can see how much they resembled each other!

Mussaurus data

Let's take another look at what is known about **Mussaurus**'s body structure. It was, of course, a prosauropod and lived during Triassic times.

Long neck

One of **Mussaurus**'s main features was a long, flexible neck. With this neck, **Mussaurus** could turn easily to look behind when it sensed danger, to search for any straying young, or to reach up into tall trees. But its neck was not nearly as long as the necks of the sauropods that evolved during later Jurassic times.

Vegetarian diet

Mussaurus's five-fingered front limbs were ideal for pulling down leafy branches on which to feed. In Triassic times, ferns and horsetails grew abundantly near water, and **Mussaurus** would graze on these, too.

Tiny young

Scientists know from the remains they have found of several newborn **Mussaurus** that they were tiny when newly hatched and much smaller than most baby dinosaurs. Yet **Mussaurus** probably grew to be 10 feet (3 m) tall when fully mature — twenty times its birth size. If *you* grew to be twenty times the size you were when *you* were born, you would grow to be a giant 25 feet (7.6 m) tall, at least. That's more than four times the height of the average adult man!

Long tail

Mussaurus also had a long, strong tail, which it probably swished from side to side as it loped along on all fours. But whenever it chose to move around on just two back legs, as experts think it sometimes did, its tail would have swept along the ground.

Death in the nest

No one can be sure why the tiny baby **Mussaurus**, whose skeletons were found in Patagonia, died so young. Even the experts can only guess. It could be that they caught some prehistoric disease and became ill. Or maybe the weather was too hot for them. Perhaps their mother had an accident and died, so there was no one to care for the hatchlings. Or, they may even have been attacked by a predator. We *do* know, however, that they huddled together for comfort, since this is how their skeletons were found in the nest, millions of years later.

GLOSSARY

carnivores — meat-eating animals.

conifers — woody shrubs or trees that bear their seeds in cones.

evolve — to change shape or develop gradually over a long period of time.

extinct — no longer alive.

fossils — traces or remains of plants and animals found in rock.

ginkgoes — trees with showy, fan-shaped leaves and yellow fruit.

herbivores — plant-eating animals.

lava — molten rock that flows out of a volcano.

oasis — a fertile area in a dry, desertlike region.

paleontologists — scientists who study the remains of plants and animals that lived long ago.

perish — to die; to be destroyed or ruined.

predators — animals that kill other animals for food.

remains — a skeleton, bones, or dead body.

scavenge — to search for and eat dead or decaying matter.

INDEX